5 EASY ingredients

pil

Publications International, Ltd.

Microwave Cooking: Microwave ovens vary in wattage. Use the cooking times as guidelines and check for doneness before adding more time.

WARNING: Food preparation, baking and cooking involve inherent dangers: misuse of electric products, sharp electric tools, boiling water, hot stoves, allergic reactions, foodborne illnesses and the like, pose numerous potential risks. Publications International, Ltd. (PIL) assumes no responsibility or liability for any damages you may experience as a result of following recipes, instructions, tips or advice in this publication.

While we hope this publication helps you find new ways to eat delicious foods, you may not always achieve the results desired due to variations in ingredients, cooking temperatures, typos, errors, omissions or individual cooking abilities.

Let's get social!

@Publications_International

@PublicationsInternational

www.pilbooks.com

Contents

BBQ CHICKEN FLATBREAD

makes 4 servings

3 tablespoons red wine vinegar

2 teaspoons sugar

¼ red onion, thinly sliced (about ⅓ cup)

3 cups shredded rotisserie chicken

½ cup barbecue sauce

1 package (about 14 ounces) refrigerated pizza dough

All-purpose flour, for dusting

1½ cups (6 ounces) shredded mozzarella cheese

1 green onion, thinly sliced diagonally

2 tablespoons chopped fresh cilantro

1. Preheat oven to 400°F. Line large baking sheet with parchment paper.

2. For pickled onion, combine vinegar and sugar in small bowl; stir until sugar is dissolved. Add red onion; cover and let stand at room temperature while preparing flatbread. Combine chicken and barbecue sauce in medium bowl; toss to coat.

3. Roll out dough into 11×9-inch rectangle on lightly floured surface. Transfer dough to prepared baking sheet; top with cheese and barbecue chicken mixture.

4. Bake 12 minutes or until crust is golden brown and cheese is melted. Drain red onion. Sprinkle red onion, green onions and cilantro over flatbread. Serve immediately.

CHICKEN & BISCUITS

makes 4 to 6 servings

¼ cup (½ stick) butter

4 boneless skinless chicken breasts (about 1¼ pounds), cut into ½-inch pieces

½ cup chopped onion

½ teaspoon dried thyme

½ teaspoon paprika

¼ teaspoon black pepper

1 can (about 14 ounces) chicken broth, divided

⅓ cup all-purpose flour

1 package (10 ounces) frozen peas and carrots

1 can (12 ounces) refrigerated buttermilk biscuits

1. Preheat oven to 375°F.

2. Melt butter in large skillet over medium heat. Add chicken, onion, thyme, paprika and pepper; cook and stir 5 minutes or until chicken is browned.

3. Combine ¼ cup broth and flour in small bowl; stir until smooth. Add remaining broth to skillet; bring to a boil. Gradually add flour mixture, whisking constantly to prevent lumps from forming. Simmer 5 minutes. Add peas and carrots; cook 2 minutes. Transfer mixture to 1½-quart casserole; top with biscuits.

4. Bake 25 to 30 minutes or until biscuits are golden brown.

TIP: Cook the chicken in an ovenproof skillet instead of the 1½-quart casserole. Place the biscuits directly on the chicken and vegetable mixture, then bake as directed.

CHIPOTLE CHICKEN ENCHILADAS

makes 8 enchiladas

- 2 cans (10 ounces each) ORTEGA® Enchilada Sauce, divided
- 2 cups shredded cooked chicken
- 1 cup ORTEGA® Refried Beans
- 1 packet (1.25 ounces) ORTEGA® Chipotle Taco Seasoning Mix
- 8 (8-inch) ORTEGA® Flour Soft Tortillas
- 1 cup (4 ounces) shredded Mexican-blend cheese

Preheat oven to 350°F. Lightly coat 13×9-inch baking dish with nonstick cooking spray. Spread ½ can enchilada sauce onto bottom of dish.

Combine chicken, 1 can enchilada sauce, beans and seasoning mix in medium skillet over medium-low heat. Cook and stir 3 to 4 minutes or until mixture is heated through.

Wrap tortillas with clean, lightly moistened cloth or paper towels. Microwave on HIGH (100% power) 1 minute, or until hot and pliable. Spoon chicken mixture evenly down center of each tortilla; roll up. Place in prepared dish, seam side down. Top evenly with remaining ½ can enchilada sauce and cheese.

Bake 15 to 20 minutes or until heated through and cheese is melted. Serve warm.

CHICKEN CAESAR SALAD

makes 2 servings

¼ cup plus 1 tablespoon Caesar salad dressing, divided

6 ounces chicken tenders, cut in half lengthwise and then crosswise

Black pepper

4 cups (about 5 ounces) Italian salad blend (romaine and radicchio)

½ cup croutons, divided

2 tablespoons grated Parmesan cheese

1. Heat 1 tablespoon salad dressing in large nonstick skillet over medium heat. Add chicken; cook and stir 3 to 4 minutes or until cooked through. Remove from skillet; season with pepper. Set aside to cool.

2. Combine salad blend, ¼ cup croutons, remaining ¼ cup salad dressing and cheese in large bowl; toss to coat. Top with chicken and remaining ¼ cup croutons.

GARLICKY OVEN-FRIED CHICKEN THIGHS

makes 4 servings

1 egg

2 tablespoons water

1 cup plain dry bread crumbs

1 teaspoon salt

1 teaspoon garlic powder

½ teaspoon black pepper

¼ teaspoon ground red pepper

8 chicken thighs (about 3 pounds)

Olive oil cooking spray

1. Preheat oven to 350°F.

2. Beat egg with water in shallow bowl. Combine bread crumbs, salt, garlic powder, black pepper and red pepper in separate shallow bowl.

3. Dip chicken into egg mixture; turn to coat. Transfer to bread crumb mixture; press lightly to coat both sides. Place, skin side up, on large baking sheet.

4. Lightly spray chicken with cooking spray. Bake 50 to 60 minutes or until browned and cooked through (165°F). *Do not turn chicken during cooking.*

VARIATIONS: Substitute your favorite dried herbs or spices for the garlic powder and ground red pepper.

CURRIED TURKEY NOODLE SOUP

makes 5 servings

1 tablespoon olive oil

¾ pound turkey breast tenderloin, cut into 1-inch pieces

5 cups water

2 packages (3 ounces each) chicken-flavored ramen noodles

1 tablespoon curry powder

1 cup sliced celery

1 medium apple, cored and chopped (1½ cups)

¼ cup dry roasted unsalted peanuts

1. Heat oil in large saucepan over medium-high heat. Add turkey; cook and stir 3 to 4 minutes or until no longer pink. Remove turkey; set aside.

2. Add water, seasoning packets from noodles and curry powder to saucepan. Bring to a boil. Reduce heat; cover and simmer 5 minutes.

3. Break up noodles; gently stir noodles and celery into saucepan. Bring mixture to a boil. Reduce heat to low. Simmer, uncovered, 5 minutes.

4. Stir in turkey and apple; cook until heated through. Ladle into soup bowls. Sprinkle with peanuts.

CREAMY TURKEY POT PIE

makes 4 servings

1 tablespoon vegetable oil

1 medium onion, chopped (about ½ cup)

1 can (10½ ounces) Campbell's® Condensed Cream of Chicken Soup or Campbell's® Condensed 98% Fat Free Cream of Chicken Soup or Campbell's® Condensed Healthy Request® Cream of Chicken Soup

½ cup milk

1 package (10 ounces) frozen peas and carrots

2 cups shredded or cubed cooked turkey or chicken

1 package (10 ounces) Pepperidge Farm® Puff Pastry Shells, prepared according to package directions

1. Heat the oil in a 10-inch skillet over medium-high heat. Add the onion and cook until tender, stirring occasionally.

2. Stir the soup, milk and peas and carrots in the skillet and heat to a boil. Reduce the heat to low. Cover and cook for 5 minutes or until the vegetables are tender. Stir in the turkey and cook until the mixture is hot and bubbling. Spoon the turkey mixture into the pastry shells. Top with the pastry "tops", if desired.

CHICKEN WITH ROSEMARY-PEACH GLAZE

makes 4 servings

4 boneless skinless chicken breasts (about 1 pound)

2 tablespoons soy sauce, divided

⅓ cup peach preserves

1 sprig fresh rosemary *or* 1 teaspoon dried rosemary

1 tablespoon lemon juice

1 clove garlic, minced

2 cups cooked wild rice and long grain rice mix

1. Preheat broiler. Spray large baking sheet with nonstick cooking spray. Sprinkle chicken with 1 tablespoon soy sauce; place on prepared baking sheet. Broil 4 to 6 inches from heat 3 minutes; turn and broil 3 minutes.

2. Meanwhile, combine preserves, rosemary, lemon juice, remaining 1 tablespoon soy sauce and garlic in small saucepan. Cook over medium-low heat 5 minutes.

3. Brush sauce over chicken; broil 2 minutes. Turn and brush with sauce. Broil 2 minutes or until chicken is no longer pink in center. Discard any remaining sauce. Serve chicken with rice.

BEER OVEN-FRIED CHICKEN

makes 4 servings

1⅓ cups light-colored beer, such as pale ale

2 tablespoons buttermilk

1¼ cups panko bread crumbs

½ cup grated Parmesan cheese

4 chicken breast cutlets (about 1¼ pounds)

½ teaspoon salt

¼ teaspoon black pepper

1. Preheat oven to 400°F. Line large baking sheet with foil.

2. Combine beer and buttermilk in shallow bowl. Combine panko and cheese in another shallow bowl.

3. Sprinkle chicken with salt and pepper. Dip in beer mixture; roll in panko mixture to coat. Place on prepared baking sheet.

4. Bake 25 to 30 minutes or until chicken is no longer pink in center.

TIP: To make a substitution for buttermilk, place 1 teaspoon lemon juice or distilled white vinegar in a measuring cup and add enough milk to measure 2 tablespoons. Stir and let the mixture stand at room temperature for 5 minutes.

CHUNKY CHICKEN STEW

makes 2 servings

1 teaspoon olive oil

1 small onion, chopped

1 cup thinly sliced carrots

1 cup chicken broth

1 can (about 14 ounces) diced tomatoes

1 cup diced cooked chicken breast

3 cups sliced kale or baby spinach

1. Heat oil in large saucepan over medium-high heat. Add onion; cook and stir 5 minutes or until golden brown. Stir in carrots and broth; bring to a boil. Reduce heat to low. Simmer, uncovered, 5 minutes.

2. Stir in tomatoes; simmer 5 minutes or until carrots are tender. Add chicken; cook and stir until heated through. Add kale; stir until wilted.

BLUE CHEESE STUFFED CHICKEN BREASTS

makes 4 servings

½ cup crumbled blue cheese

2 tablespoons butter, softened and divided

¾ teaspoon dried thyme

Salt and black pepper

4 bone-in skin-on chicken breasts

1 tablespoon lemon juice

1. Preheat oven to 400°F. Combine cheese, 1 tablespoon butter and thyme in small bowl; mix well. Season with salt and pepper.

2. Loosen chicken skin by pushing fingers between skin and meat, taking care not to tear skin. Spread cheese mixture under skin; massage skin to spread mixture evenly over chicken breasts. Place in shallow roasting pan.

3. Melt remaining 1 tablespoon butter in small bowl; stir in lemon juice until blended. Brush mixture over chicken. Sprinkle with salt and pepper.

4. Roast 50 minutes or until chicken is cooked through (165°F).

CHICKEN BACON QUESADILLAS

makes 4 servings

4 teaspoons vegetable oil, divided

4 (8-inch) flour tortillas

1 cup (4 ounces) shredded Colby-Jack cheese

2 cups coarsely chopped cooked chicken

4 slices bacon, crisp-cooked and coarsely chopped

½ cup pico de gallo, plus additional for serving

Sour cream and guacamole (optional)

1. Heat large nonstick skillet over medium heat; brush with 1 teaspoon oil. Place one tortilla in skillet; sprinkle with ¼ cup cheese. Spread ½ cup chicken over one half of tortilla; top with one fourth of bacon and 2 tablespoons pico de gallo.

2. Cook 1 to 2 minutes or until cheese is melted and bottom of tortilla is lightly browned. Fold tortilla over filling, pressing with spatula. Remove to large cutting board; cool slightly. Cut into wedges. Repeat with remaining ingredients. Serve with additional pico de gallo, sour cream and guacamole, if desired.

CHICKEN ADOBO

makes 6 servings

½ cup cider vinegar

½ cup soy sauce

4 cloves garlic, minced

3 bay leaves

1 teaspoon black pepper

2½ pounds bone-in skin-on chicken thighs (about 6)

Hot cooked rice (optional)

Sliced green onion (optional)

1. Combine vinegar, soy sauce, garlic, bay leaves and pepper in large saucepan or deep skillet; mix well. Add chicken; turn to coat. Arrange chicken skin side down in liquid.

2. Bring to a boil over high heat. Reduce heat to low. Cover; simmer 30 minutes. Turn chicken skin side up. Cook, uncovered, 20 minutes. Preheat broiler. Line large baking sheet with foil.

3. Remove chicken to prepared baking sheet, skin side up. Broil 6 minutes or until skin is browned and crisp. Meanwhile, cook liquid in saucepan over high heat 10 minutes or until reduced and slightly thickened.

4. Serve sauce over chicken and rice, if desired. Garnish with green onion.

SIZZLING CHICKEN AND VEGGIE FAJITAS

makes 6 servings

1 pound boneless skinless chicken thighs, cut crosswise into strips

1 teaspoon dried oregano

1 teaspoon chili powder

½ teaspoon garlic salt

2 bell peppers (preferably 1 red and 1 green), cut into thin strips

4 thin slices large sweet or yellow onion, separated into rings

½ cup salsa

6 (6-inch) flour tortillas, warmed

½ cup chopped fresh cilantro or green onions

Sour cream (optional)

1. Toss chicken with oregano, chili powder and garlic salt in large bowl. Heat large skillet coated with nonstick cooking spray over medium-high heat. Add chicken; cook and stir 5 to 6 minutes or until cooked through. Remove to large bowl; set aside.

2. Add bell peppers and onion to same skillet; cook and stir 2 minutes over medium heat. Add salsa; cover and cook 6 to 8 minutes or until vegetables are tender. Uncover; stir in chicken and any juices from bowl. Cook and stir 2 minutes or until heated through.

3. Serve mixture on top of tortillas topped with cilantro and sour cream, if desired.

CHICKEN ROLL-UPS

makes 4 servings

2½ cups marinara sauce, divided

4 boneless skinless chicken breasts (about ¼ pound each)

2 cups fresh baby spinach leaves

4 slices (1 ounce each) mozzarella cheese

¼ cup grated Parmesan cheese

Red pepper flakes (optional)

1. Preheat oven to 400°F. Spray 2-quart baking dish with nonstick cooking spray. Spread 1 cup marinara sauce on bottom of dish.

2. Place 1 chicken breast between two sheets of plastic wrap on large cutting board. Pound with rolling pin until meat is about ¼ inch thick. Repeat with remaining chicken.

3. Place ½ cup spinach on each chicken breast. Top with mozzarella cheese slices. Roll up tightly. Place rolls, seam side down, in prepared dish. Top with remaining 1½ cups marinara sauce.

4. Cover dish with foil; bake 35 minutes. Uncover; bake 10 minutes. Sprinkle with Parmesan cheese and red pepper flakes, if desired.

AWESOME GRILLED CHEESE SANDWICHES

makes 3 servings

1 package (11.25 ounces) Pepperidge Farm® Garlic Texas Toast

6 slices fontina cheese or mozzarella cheese

6 thin slices deli smoked turkey

3 thin slices prosciutto

1 jar (12 ounces) sliced roasted red pepper, drained

1. Heat a panini or sandwich press according to the manufacturer's directions until hot. (Or, use a cast-iron skillet or ridged grill pan.)

2. Top **3** of the bread slices with **half** of the cheese, turkey, prosciutto, peppers and remaining cheese. Top with the remaining bread slices.

3. Put the sandwiches on the press, closing the lid onto the sandwiches. Cook the sandwiches for 5 minutes (if cooking in a skillet or grill pan, press with a spatula occasionally or weigh down with another cast-iron skillet), until lightly browned and the bread is crisp and the cheese melts.

KITCHEN TIP: For a spicier flavor, add a dash of crushed red pepper flakes on the cheese when assembling the sandwiches.

CHICKEN TORTILLA SOUP

makes 5 servings

2 tablespoons canola oil

½ cup finely chopped onion

½ cup finely chopped carrot

2½ cups shredded cooked rotisserie chicken

1 cup thick and chunky salsa

4 cups chicken broth

1 tablespoon lime juice

1 avocado, chopped

10 corn tortilla chips, broken into thirds

1. Heat oil in large saucepan over high heat. Add onion and carrot; cook and stir 3 minutes or until onion is translucent.

2. Stir in chicken and salsa. Add broth; bring to a boil. Reduce heat to medium-low. Cover; simmer 5 minutes or until carrot is crisp-tender. Remove from heat; stir in lime juice.

3. Top with avocado and tortilla chips just before serving.

COBB SALAD

makes 4 servings

1 package (10 ounces) torn mixed salad greens *or* 8 cups torn romaine lettuce

6 ounces cooked chicken breast, cut into 1-inch pieces

1 tomato, seeded and chopped

2 hard-cooked eggs, cut into 1-inch pieces

4 slices bacon, crisp-cooked and crumbled

1 ripe avocado, diced

1 large carrot, shredded

½ cup blue cheese, crumbled

Blue cheese dressing (optional)

1. Place greens in large serving bowl. Arrange chicken, tomato, eggs, bacon, avocado, carrot and cheese on top of lettuce.

2. Serve with dressing, if desired.

FRENCH DIP SANDWICHES

makes 6 servings

3 pounds boneless beef chuck roast

½ teaspoon salt

½ teaspoon black pepper

1 tablespoon olive oil

2 large onions, cut into halves, then cut into ¼-inch slices

2¼ cups beef broth, divided

3 tablespoons Worcestershire sauce

6 hoagie rolls, split

12 slices provolone cheese

1. Season beef with salt and pepper. Heat oil in Dutch oven or large saucepan over medium-high heat. Add beef; cook 6 minutes per side or until browned. Remove to plate.

2. Add onions and ¼ cup broth to Dutch oven; cook 8 minutes or until golden brown, stirring occasionally and scraping up browned bits from bottom of pot. Remove half of onions to small bowl; set aside. Stir in remaining 2 cups broth and Worcestershire sauce; mix well. Return beef to Dutch oven. Reduce heat to low. Cover; cook 3 to 3½ hours or until beef is fork-tender.

3. Remove beef to large bowl; let stand until cool enough to handle. Shred into bite-size pieces. Add ⅔ cup cooking liquid; toss to coat. Pour remaining cooking liquid into small bowl for serving. Preheat broiler. Line baking sheet with foil.

4. Place rolls cut side up on prepared baking sheet; broil until lightly browned. Top bottom halves of rolls with cheese, beef and reserved onions. Serve with warm au jus for dipping.

OVERSTUFFED MEXICAN-STYLE PEPPERS

makes 4 servings

10 ounces ground beef

½ cup finely chopped onion

1 can (about 4 ounces) chopped mild green chiles

½ cup corn

½ cup tomato sauce, divided

¼ cup cornmeal

½ teaspoon salt

½ teaspoon ground cumin

2 large green bell peppers, cut in half lengthwise, seeded and stemmed (about 8 ounces each)

⅔ cup (about 2½ ounces) shredded sharp Cheddar cheese

1. Preheat oven to 375°F.

2. Brown beef in large skillet over medium-high heat 6 to 8 minutes, stirring to break up meat. Drain fat. Add onion, chiles, corn, ¼ cup tomato sauce, cornmeal, salt and cumin; mix well.

3. Arrange pepper halves, cut side up, in 12×8-inch baking pan. Spoon beef mixture evenly into each pepper half. Spoon remaining ¼ cup tomato sauce over beef mixture.

4. Bake 35 minutes or until peppers are tender. Sprinkle evenly with cheese. Serve immediately.

TIP: To freeze, place each pepper half in large resealable food storage bags. Release any excess air from bags and seal. Freeze bags flat for easier storage and faster thawing. To reheat, open the food storage bag and place on a microwavable plate. Microwave on HIGH 3 to 3½ minutes or until warm. Remove from bag and place on plate.

BBQ BEEF PIZZA

makes 3 to 4 servings

½ pound ground beef

¾ cup prepared barbecue sauce

1 medium green bell pepper

1 (14-inch) prepared pizza crust

3 to 4 onion slices, separated into rings

½ (2¼-ounce) can sliced black olives, drained

1 cup (4 ounces) shredded Colby-Jack cheese

1. Preheat oven to 400°F. Brown beef in large skillet over medium-high heat 6 to 8 minutes, stirring to separate meat. Drain fat. Stir in barbecue sauce.

2. Meanwhile, seed bell pepper and slice into ¼-inch-thick rings. Place pizza crust on large baking pan. Spread meat mixture over pizza crust to within ½ inch of edge. Arrange onion slices and pepper rings over meat. Sprinkle with olives and cheese. Bake 8 minutes or until cheese is melted. Cut into eight wedges.

Beef

BEEF TENDERLOIN WITH LEMON BUTTER

makes 2 servings

2 beef tenderloin (filet mignon) steaks (6 ounces each)

¼ teaspoon salt, divided

⅛ teaspoon black pepper

⅛ teaspoon garlic powder

3 tablespoons butter, softened, divided

1 tablespoon finely minced parsley

¾ teaspoon grated lemon peel

⅛ to ¼ teaspoon dried tarragon, crushed

1 tablespoon canola oil

1. Sprinkle both sides of beef with ⅛ teaspoon salt, pepper and garlic powder. Set aside 15 minutes.

2. Meanwhile, combine 2 tablespoons butter, parsley, lemon peel, tarragon and remaining ⅛ teaspoon salt in small bowl; mix well.

3. Heat remaining 1 tablespoon butter and oil in medium skillet over medium-high heat until bubbly. Add beef; cook 2 minutes per side. Reduce heat to medium. Cook 3 minutes per side or until desired doneness. Top steaks with lemon butter.

SLOPPY JOE CASSEROLE

makes 5 servings

1 pound ground beef

1 can (10¾ ounces)
Campbell's®
Condensed Tomato
Soup (Regular or
Healthy Request®)

¼ cup water

1 teaspoon Worcestershire
sauce

⅛ teaspoon ground black
pepper

1 package (7.5 ounces)
refrigerated biscuits
(10 biscuits)

½ cup shredded
Cheddar cheese
(about 2 ounces)

1. Heat the oven to 400°F.

2. Cook the beef in a 10-inch skillet over medium-high heat until well browned, stirring often to separate the meat. Pour off any fat.

3. Stir the soup, water, Worcestershire and black pepper in the skillet and heat to a boil. Spoon the beef mixture into a 1½-quart casserole. Arrange the biscuits around the inside edge of the casserole.

4. Bake for 15 minutes or until the biscuits are golden brown. Sprinkle the cheese over the beef mixture.

KITCHEN TIP: Sharp **or** mild Cheddar cheese will work in this recipe.

Beef

SPICY CHINESE PEPPER STEAK

makes 4 servings

1 boneless beef top sirloin steak (about 1 pound) or tenderloin tips, cut into thin strips

1 tablespoon cornstarch

3 cloves garlic, minced

½ teaspoon red pepper flakes

2 tablespoons peanut or canola oil, divided

1 green bell pepper, cut into thin strips

1 red bell pepper, cut into thin strips

¼ cup oyster sauce

2 tablespoons soy sauce

3 tablespoons chopped fresh cilantro or green onions

1. Combine beef, cornstarch, garlic and red pepper flakes in medium bowl; toss to coat.

2. Heat 1 tablespoon oil in wok or large skillet over medium-high heat. Add bell peppers; stir-fry 3 minutes. Remove to small bowl. Add remaining 1 tablespoon oil and beef mixture to wok; stir-fry 4 to 5 minutes or until beef is barely pink in center.

3. Add oyster sauce and soy sauce to wok; cook and stir 1 minute. Return bell peppers to wok; cook and stir 1 to 2 minutes or until sauce thickens. Sprinkle with cilantro.

GRILLED BEEF AND PINEAPPLE KABOBS

makes 4 servings

1 boneless beef top sirloin or top round steak (about 1 pound)

1 small onion, finely chopped

½ cup teriyaki sauce

16 pieces (1-inch cubes) fresh pineapple

1 can (8 ounces) water chestnuts, drained

1. Prepare grill for direct cooking. Cut steak into 1-inch-pieces. For marinade, combine onion and teriyaki sauce in small bowl. Add beef to marinade, stirring to coat.

2. Alternately thread beef, pineapple cubes and water chestnuts onto four bamboo or thin metal skewers. (If using bamboo skewers, soak in water 20 to 30 minutes before using to prevent them from burning.)

3. Place kabobs on grid over medium coals. Grill 4 minutes, turning once, or until meat is cooked through. Serve immediately.

NOTE: Recipe can also be prepared with flank steak.

SERVING SUGGESTION: Serve with hot cooked rice and stir-fried broccoli, mushrooms and red bell peppers.

Beef

BEEF TACO SALAD WITH GUACAMOLE DRESSING

makes 6 servings

- 1 tablespoon olive oil
- 1 cup chopped onion
- 1 pound lean ground beef
- ¾ cup water
- 1 ORTEGA® Whole Grain Corn Taco Kit—includes 10 taco shells, 1 packet (1.25 ounces) taco seasoning mix and 1 packet (3 ounces) taco sauce
- 1 head iceberg lettuce, diced
- 2 cups halved cherry tomatoes
- 2 cups (8 ounces) shredded Cheddar cheese
- ½ cup ORTEGA® Guacamole Style Dip
- ¼ cup mayonnaise

Heat olive oil in medium skillet over medium heat. Add onions; cook and stir 4 minutes or until translucent. Add beef; cook and stir 5 minutes or until no longer pink. Drain and discard fat. Stir in water; add seasoning mix and taco sauce from Taco Kit; mix well. Cook and stir 5 to 6 minutes or until thickened.

Break taco shells from Taco Kit into bite-sized pieces in large salad bowl. Add lettuce, tomatoes and cheese; toss to combine. Add meat mixture; toss to combine.

Combine guacamole dip and mayonnaise in small bowl; pour over salad. Toss lightly. Serve warm salad immediately.

TIP: For more color and nutrition, add other fresh vegetables to the salad, including shredded carrots, sliced radishes, sliced cucumbers or broccoli florets.

CHILI CHEESE FRIES

makes 4 servings

1½ pounds ground beef

1 medium onion, chopped

2 cloves garlic, minced

½ cup lager

2 tablespoons chili powder

2 tablespoons tomato paste

Salt and black pepper

1 package (32 ounces) frozen French fries

1 jar (15 ounces) cheese sauce, heated

Sour cream and chopped green onions (optional)

1. Brown beef, onion and garlic in large skillet over medium-high heat 6 to 8 minutes, stirring to break up meat. Drain fat.

2. Stir lager, chili powder and tomato paste into beef mixture. Simmer, stirring occasionally, 20 minutes or until most liquid has evaporated. Season with salt and pepper.

3. Meanwhile, bake French fries according to package directions.

4. Divide French fries evenly among bowls. Top evenly with chili and cheese sauce. Garnish with sour cream and green onions.

THE ROYAL BURGER

makes 2 servings

1 teaspoon Royal Seasoning (recipe follows), divided

4 slices bacon

12 ounces ground beef

2 slices deli American cheese

2 eggs
Salt and black pepper

2 sesame seed buns, split and toasted

2 tablespoons mayonnaise

½ cup shredded lettuce

2 slices ripe tomato

1. Prepare Royal Seasoning.

2. Cook bacon in large skillet over medium heat; drain on paper towel-lined plate. Pour off all but 1 teaspoon drippings from skillet. (Reserve some of bacon drippings for frying eggs, if desired.)

3. Combine beef and ¾ teaspoon Royal Seasoning in medium bowl; mix gently. Shape into 2 (5-inch) patties. Sprinkle both sides of patties with remaining ¼ teaspoon seasoning mix.

4. Return skillet to medium heat. Cook patties about 5 minutes per side or until cooked through (160°F).* Top each burger with cheese slice during last minute of cooking.

5. While burgers are cooking, heat 2 teaspoons reserved bacon drippings or butter in another large skillet or griddle over medium heat. Crack eggs into skillet; cook 3 to 4 minutes or until whites are set and yolks begin to thicken and firm around edges. Season with salt and pepper.

6. Spread cut sides of buns with mayonnaise. Top bottom buns with lettuce, burgers, bacon, tomato, eggs and top buns.

*Patties can also be grilled or broiled 5 minutes per side or until cooked through.

ROYAL SEASONING

makes about ⅓ cup

- 2 tablespoons salt
- 1½ tablespoons paprika
- 1 tablespoon garlic powder
- ½ tablespoon onion powder
- ½ tablespoon chili powder
- ¾ teaspoon ground cumin
- ¾ teaspoon dried basil
- ¾ teaspoon black pepper
- ¼ teaspoon dried oregano

Combine salt, paprika, garlic powder, onion powder, chili powder, cumin, basil, pepper and oregano in small bowl; mix well. Store in airtight container.

NOTE: Seasoning mix can be used for steaks, chicken and vegetables in addition to burgers.

Beef

POTATO AND CORNED BEEF CAKES

makes 10 cakes

2 pounds russet potatoes, divided

2 teaspoons salt, divided

6 tablespoons all-purpose flour

¼ cup whole milk

1 egg, beaten

½ teaspoon black pepper

1 cup chopped corned beef (leftover or deli corned beef, about ⅓ pound, cut into ¼-inch pieces)

1 tablespoon butter

1 tablespoon olive oil

Chopped fresh parsley (optional)

1. Peel half of potatoes; cut into 1-inch pieces. Place in medium saucepan; add 1 teaspoon salt and water to cover by 2 inches. Bring to a simmer over medium heat; cook 15 minutes or until tender. Drain potatoes; rice into medium bowl.

2. Peel remaining half of potatoes; grate with box grater. Squeeze out and discard liquid from grated potatoes. Add grated potatoes to riced potatoes in bowl; stir in flour, milk, egg, remaining 1 teaspoon salt and pepper. Stir in corned beef until well blended.

3. Heat butter and oil in large skillet (preferably cast iron) over medium heat. Shape ⅓ cupfuls of potato mixture into patties; cook in batches 3 to 4 minutes per side or until golden brown. (Do not crowd patties in skillet.) Sprinkle with parsley, if desired.

Beef

SLOW-COOKED MEXICAN BRISKET

makes 4 servings

2 large onions, diced (about 4 cups)

1 (3- to 4-pound) beef brisket

1 can (4 ounces) ORTEGA® Fire-Roasted Diced Green Chilies

2 jars (16 ounces each) ORTEGA® Salsa, any variety

1 teaspoon cornstarch

SLOW COOKER DIRECTIONS

Place onions in large slow cooker; top with brisket. Combine chilies, 2 jars salsa and 1 salsa jar of water in large bowl; pour over brisket. Cover and cook on LOW for 8 hours or HIGH for 4 hours.

Remove brisket to cutting board. Cover with foil to keep warm. Pour sauce from slow cooker into large skillet. Heat over medium-high heat until bubbly. Reduce heat and simmer 10 minutes or until thickened.

Remove 1 cup sauce and place in small bowl; add cornstarch, stirring until cornstarch has dissolved. Return mixture to skillet and cook several minutes until thickened.

Thinly slice brisket and serve with sauce.

TIP: The brisket goes well with a side of rice or noodles, and some sauce on top.

Beef

BARBECUE BEEF SANDWICHES

makes 4 servings

2½ pounds boneless beef chuck roast

2 tablespoons Southwest seasoning

1 tablespoon vegetable oil

1¼ cups beef broth

2½ cups barbecue sauce, divided

4 sandwich or pretzel buns, split

1⅓ cups prepared coleslaw* (preferably vinegar based)

1. Sprinkle both sides of beef with Southwest seasoning. Heat oil in Dutch oven over medium-high heat. Add beef; cook 6 minutes per side or until browned. Remove to plate.

2. Add broth; cook 2 minutes, scraping up browned bits from bottom of Dutch oven. Stir in 2 cups barbecue sauce; bring to a boil. Return beef to Dutch oven; turn to coat.

3. Reduce heat to low. Cover; cook 3 to 3½ hours or until beef is fork-tender, turning beef halfway through cooking time.

4. Remove beef to large plate; let stand until cool enough to handle. Meanwhile, cook sauce remaining in Dutch oven over high heat 10 minutes or until reduced and slightly thickened.

5. Shred beef into bite-size pieces. Stir in 1 cup reduced cooking sauce and ¼ cup barbecue sauce. Add remaining ¼ cup barbecue sauce, if desired. Fill buns with beef mixture; top with coleslaw.

Beef

MINI MARINATED BEEF SKEWERS

makes 6 servings

1 boneless beef top round steak (about 1 pound)

2 tablespoons soy sauce

1 tablespoon dry sherry

1 teaspoon dark sesame oil

2 cloves garlic, minced

18 fresh greens and halved cherry tomatoes (optional)

1. Cut beef crosswise into 18 (⅛-inch-thick) slices. Place in large resealable food storage bag. Add soy sauce, sherry, oil and garlic. Seal bag; turn to coat. Marinate in refrigerator at least 30 minutes or up to 2 hours.

2. Meanwhile, soak 18 (6-inch) wooden skewers in water 20 minutes.

3. Preheat broiler. Drain beef; discard marinade. Weave beef accordion-style onto skewers. Place on rack of broiler pan.

4. Broil 4 to 5 inches from heat 2 minutes. Turn skewers over; broil 2 minutes or until beef is barely pink. Serve warm with greens and tomatoes, if desired.

Beef

BEEF & SALSA SALAD SUPREME

makes 4 servings

1 boneless beef top sirloin steak (about 1 pound)

2 teaspoons Mexican seasoning blend or chili powder

1 package (8 ounces) assorted torn salad greens

1 cup canned black beans, rinsed and drained

1 cup frozen corn, thawed

¼ cup salsa or picante sauce

¼ cup red wine vinegar and oil salad dressing

1 medium tomato, chopped

1. Heat large nonstick skillet over medium heat. Rub both sides of steak with Mexican seasoning. Cook steak in skillet 5 minutes per side to medium rare or until desired doneness. Remove steak to large cutting board; tent with foil. Let stand 5 minutes.

2. Meanwhile, combine salad greens, beans and corn in large bowl. Combine salsa and dressing in small bowl; pour over greens mixture. Toss lightly to coat. Evenly divide on salad plates.

3. Carve steak crosswise into ¼-inch-thick strips; arrange over salad greens, dividing evenly. Sprinkle with tomato.

SERVING SUGGESTION: For a special touch, add a sprig of cilantro to each serving.

Beef

SHREDDED BEEF FAJITAS

makes 6 servings

1 beef flank steak (about 1 pound)

1 can (about 14 ounces) diced tomatoes with mild green chiles, undrained

1 cup chopped onion

½ medium green bell pepper, cut into ½-inch pieces

1 clove garlic, minced *or* ¼ teaspoon garlic powder

½ package (about 2 tablespoons) fajita seasoning mix

6 (8-inch) flour tortillas

Optional toppings: chopped cilantro, guacamole, shredded Cheddar cheese and/or salsa

SLOW COOKER DIRECTIONS

1. Cut beef into six portions; place in 3½-quart slow cooker. Combine tomatoes with juice, onion, bell pepper, garlic and fajita seasoning mix in medium bowl. Pour over beef. Cover; cook on LOW 8 to 10 hours or on HIGH 4 to 5 hours.

2. Remove beef to large cutting board; shred with two forks. Stir beef back into slow cooker.

3. To serve fajitas, place beef mixture evenly into tortillas. Top as desired; fold tortillas over beef mixture.

Beef

BEEF & TURKEY MEAT LOAF

makes 8 servings

¾ pound ground beef

¾ pound ground turkey

½ cup grated carrot

⅓ cup finely chopped onion

⅓ cup crushed corn or rice cereal squares

⅓ cup plus 2 tablespoons chili sauce, divided

1 egg, beaten

¾ teaspoon salt

½ teaspoon black pepper

1. Preheat oven to 350°F.

2. Combine beef, turkey, carrot, onion, cereal, ⅓ cup chili sauce, egg, salt and pepper in large bowl; mix well.

3. Shape into 8-inch-long loaf in 13×9-inch pan. Spread remaining 2 tablespoons chili sauce evenly over top of meat loaf.

4. Bake 1 hour and 15 minutes or until cooked through (165°F).

SWISS STEAK

makes 6 servings

1½ pounds top round steak, well trimmed (½ inch thick)

½ teaspoon salt

¼ teaspoon black pepper

3 tablespoons all-purpose flour

2 teaspoons olive oil

½ cup chopped onion

1 stalk celery, sliced

1 can (about 14 ounces) diced tomatoes with garlic, basil and oregano, undrained

½ cup diced green bell pepper

½ cup beef broth

1. Cut beef into six equal pieces. Pound beef* on both sides with meat mallet. Combine salt and black pepper in small bowl; sprinkle about half of salt mixture over beef. Place flour in large resealable food storage bag. Add beef, two pieces at a time; shake to coat with flour.

2. Heat oil in large skillet over medium-high heat. Brown beef 3 to 4 minutes on both sides; remove from skillet. Add onion and celery to skillet; cook and stir 3 to 4 minutes over medium heat.

3. Add tomatoes with juice, bell pepper and broth; bring to a boil. Return beef to skillet. Reduce heat to low. Cover and simmer 1 hour or until beef is tender.

*Some supermarkets offer mechanically tenderized bottom round steak. For tenderized steak, omit pounding in step 1.

CREAMY PORK MARSALA WITH FETTUCCINE

makes 4 servings

1 tablespoon olive oil

4 boneless pork chops, ¾-inch thick (about 1 pound)

1 cup sliced mushrooms (about 3 ounces)

1 clove garlic, minced

1 can (10¾ ounces) Campbell's® Condensed Cream of Mushroom Soup (Regular **or** 98% Fat Free)

½ cup milk

2 tablespoons dry Marsala wine

8 ounces spinach fettuccine, cooked and drained

1. Heat the oil in a 10-inch skillet over medium-high heat. Add the pork and cook until well browned on both sides.

2. Reduce the heat to medium. Add the mushrooms and garlic to the skillet and cook until the mushrooms are tender.

3. Stir the soup, milk and wine in the skillet and heat to a boil. Reduce the heat to low. Cover and cook for 5 minutes or until the pork is cooked through. Serve the pork and sauce with the pasta.

KITCHEN TIP: Marsalas can range from dry to sweet, so be sure to use a dry one for this recipe.

KALUA PIG

makes 6 servings

3 slices bacon

1½ tablespoons coarse sea salt

1 boneless pork shoulder roast (5 to 6 pounds)

1 tablespoon liquid smoke

SLOW COOKER DIRECTIONS

1. Line slow cooker with bacon. Rub salt generously over pork; place on top of bacon. Pour liquid smoke over pork.

2. Cover; cook on LOW 16 to 18 hours. Remove pork to large cutting board; shred with two forks. *Do not shred pork in cooking liquid.*

SERVING SUGGESTIONS: Serve with hot cooked rice with green onion and chopped fresh cilantro, cabbage and/or fresh pineapple wedges.

SEASONED BABY BACK RIBS

makes 6 servings

1 tablespoon paprika

1½ teaspoons garlic salt

1 teaspoon celery salt

½ teaspoon black pepper

¼ teaspoon ground red pepper

4 pounds pork baby back ribs, cut into 3- to 4-rib portions, well trimmed

Barbecue Sauce (recipe follows)

Orange peel (optional)

1. Preheat oven to 350°F.

2. Combine paprika, garlic salt, celery salt, black pepper and red pepper in small bowl; stir to blend. Rub over all sides of ribs.

3. Place ribs in foil-lined shallow roasting pan. Bake 30 minutes.

4. Meanwhile, prepare grill for direct cooking. Prepare Barbecue Sauce; set aside.

5. Place ribs directly on grid. Grill, covered, over medium coals 10 minutes.

6. Remove ribs from rib rack with tongs; brush half of Barbecue Sauce over both sides of ribs. Return ribs to rib rack. Continue to grill, covered, 10 minutes or until ribs are tender and browned. Serve with reserved sauce. Garnish with orange peel, if desired.

BARBECUE SAUCE

makes about ⅔ cup

½ cup ketchup

⅓ cup packed light brown sugar

1 tablespoon cider vinegar

2 teaspoons Worcestershire sauce

2 teaspoons soy sauce

Combine ketchup, brown sugar, vinegar, Worcestershire sauce and soy sauce in glass measuring cup or small bowl. Reserve half of sauce for serving.

CORN BREAD STUFFING WITH SAUSAGE AND APPLE

makes 4 servings

⅓ cup pecan pieces

1 pound bulk pork sausage

1 large Jonathan apple

1⅓ cups chicken broth

¼ cup apple juice

6 ounces seasoned corn bread stuffing mix

1. Preheat oven to 300°F. Place pecans in shallow baking pan. Bake 6 to 8 minutes or until lightly browned, stirring frequently.

2. Place sausage in large skillet; cook over high heat 10 minutes or until meat is no longer pink, stirring to break up meat. Pour off drippings.

3. Meanwhile, coarsely chop apple. Place in 3-quart saucepan. Add broth, apple juice and seasoning packet from stuffing mix. Bring to a boil, uncovered, over high heat. Remove from heat and stir in stuffing mix. Cover; let stand 3 to 5 minutes or until stuffing is moist and tender.

4. Stir sausage into stuffing. Spoon into serving bowl; top with nuts.

CLASSIC BABY BACK RIBS >>

makes about 4 servings

3 to 4 pounds pork baby back ribs, cut into 3-rib portions (2 to 3 racks)

1 cup *Cattlemen's*® Award Winning Classic Barbecue Sauce

1. Grill ribs over indirect heat on a covered grill for 1½ hours (or in a 350°F oven).

2. Baste with barbecue sauce. Cook 30 minutes longer until meat is very tender. Serve with additional barbecue sauce.

TIP: To make Blazin' BBQ Wings, mix equal amounts *Cattlemen's*® Award Winning Classic Barbecue Sauce with *Frank's*® *Redhot*® Original Cayenne Pepper Sauce and coat cooked wings.

MAPLE & SAGE PORK CHOPS

makes 4 servings

2 tablespoons finely chopped fresh sage, plus additional for garnish

2 teaspoons olive oil

½ teaspoon salt

4 boneless pork chops (about 4 ounces each)

2 teaspoons maple syrup

1. Preheat broiler. Combine 2 tablespoons sage, oil and salt in small bowl. Rub mixture evenly over pork chops. Place on rimmed baking sheet.

2. Broil pork chops 4 minutes. Turn over; brush evenly with syrup. Broil 4 minutes or until pork chops are browned and barely pink in center. Garnish with additional sage.

SERVING SUGGESTION: Serve with fresh roasted vegetables.

TERIYAKI PORK & MANGO SALSA

makes 4 servings

2 pounds pork tenderloin (2 or 3 tenderloins)

1 cup teriyaki sauce

2 large mangoes, peeled and cut into 1-inch pieces

½ red onion, minced

1 or 2 jalapeño peppers, minced

3 cloves garlic, minced

½ cup fresh cilantro, finely chopped

Juice of 2 limes

Salt

1. Place pork in large resealable food storage bag. Pour teriyaki sauce over pork; seal bag. Refrigerate 1 to 4 hours.

2. To prepare salsa, place mangoes in medium bowl. Add onion, jalapeño and garlic. Gently stir in cilantro and lime juice. Season with salt. Refrigerate until ready to serve.

3. Preheat oven to 375°F. Place pork in roasting pan; discard marinade. Roast 20 to 30 minutes or until pork is barely pink in center (160°F). Slice and serve with mango salsa.

Pork

SOUTHWEST GRILLED PORK SALAD

makes 4 servings

½ cup mayonnaise

¼ cup orange juice

1 teaspoon grated orange peel

4 teaspoons chili powder

4 boneless pork chops

8 cups baby spinach leaves

2 oranges, cut into sections

1½ cups jicama,* cut into matchsticks

1 cup FRENCH'S® French Fried Onions

Jicama is a root vegetable with a thick brown skin and crunchy, sweet flesh. It may be eaten raw or cooked. It can be purchased in most supermarkets or Mexican markets. Canned, sliced water chestnuts may be substituted.

MIX mayonnaise, juice and peel; reserve. Rub chili powder onto both sides of pork.

GRILL pork over medium-high heat until no longer pink in center; cut into cubes.

ARRANGE spinach, oranges, jicama and pork on serving plates.

SERVE with dressing and top with French Fried Onions.

Pork

ORANGE PICANTE PORK CHOPS >>

makes 4 servings

¾ cup Pace® Picante Sauce

¼ cup orange juice

¼ teaspoon garlic powder

4 boneless pork chops, ¾-inch thick

1. Mix the picante sauce, orange juice and garlic in a shallow nonmetallic dish. Add the chops and turn to coat. Cover and refrigerate for 1 hour. Remove the chops from the picante sauce mixture.

2. Lightly oil the grill rack and heat the grill to medium. Grill the chops for 15 minutes or until cooked through, turning and brushing often with picante sauce mixture. Discard remaining picante sauce mixture.

EASY MOO SHU PORK

makes 2 servings

7 ounces pork tenderloin, sliced

4 green onions, cut into ½-inch pieces

1½ cups packaged coleslaw mix

2 tablespoons hoisin sauce or Asian plum sauce

4 (8-inch) flour tortillas, warmed

1. Spray large skillet with nonstick cooking spray; heat over medium-high heat. Add pork and green onions; stir-fry 2 to 3 minutes or until pork is barely pink in center. Stir in coleslaw mix and hoisin sauce.

2. Spoon pork mixture onto tortillas. Roll up tortillas, folding in sides to enclose filling.

NOTE: To warm tortillas, stack and wrap loosely in plastic wrap. Microwave on HIGH 15 to 20 seconds or until warm and pliable.

PULLED PORK QUESADILLAS

makes 4 servings

1 pound pork tenderloin, cut into 3-inch pieces

1 cup beer

1 cup barbecue sauce

1 teaspoon chili powder

4 (8-inch) flour tortillas

2⅔ cups shredded Monterey Jack cheese

Optional toppings: salsa, sour cream and/or fresh cilantro leaves

1. Combine pork, beer, barbecue sauce and chili powder in large saucepan over medium-high heat; bring to a boil. Reduce heat to medium-low. Cover; simmer 50 minutes or until pork is tender, stirring occasionally. Remove pork to large bowl; shred using two forks.

2. Bring sauce to a boil over medium-high heat; boil 8 to 10 minutes or until thickened. Add ¾ cup sauce to shredded pork; discard remaining sauce.

3. Place tortillas on work surface. Layer bottom half of each tortilla evenly with pork and cheese. Fold top halves of tortillas over filling to form semicircle.

4. Heat large nonstick skillet over medium heat. Add two quesadillas; cook 6 to 8 minutes or until golden and cheese is melted, turning once. Remove to large cutting board. Cut each quesadilla into three wedges. Repeat with remaining quesadillas. Top as desired.

GARLIC PORK WITH ROASTED RED POTATOES

makes 4 servings

½ teaspoon paprika

½ teaspoon garlic powder

1 pound pork tenderloin

1 tablespoon extra virgin olive oil

6 unpeeled new red potatoes, scrubbed and quartered (12 ounces total)

1 teaspoon dried oregano

½ teaspoon salt

½ teaspoon black pepper

1. Preheat oven to 425°F. Spray 13×9-inch baking pan with nonstick cooking spray.

2. Combine paprika and garlic powder in small bowl; stir to blend. Sprinkle evenly over pork.

3. Spray large skillet with cooking spray; heat over medium-high heat. Cook pork 3 minutes per side or until browned. Place in center of prepared pan.

4. Remove skillet from heat. Add oil, potatoes and oregano; toss to coat. Arrange potato mixture around pork in prepared pan, scraping sides and bottom of skillet with rubber spatula. Season with salt and pepper. Bake, uncovered, 22 minutes or until pork reaches 155° to 160°F.

5. Remove pork to large cutting board; let stand 5 minutes before slicing. Stir potatoes; cover with foil and let stand while pork is resting. Serve pork with potatoes.

CHIPOTLE PORK TACO CUPS

makes 10 servings

Vegetable cooking spray

10 whole wheat **or** flour tortillas (6-inch)

1 container (18 ounces) refrigerated cooked barbecue sauce with shredded pork (about 2 cups)

1 cup Pace® Picante Sauce

¼ teaspoon ground chipotle chile pepper

Shredded Cheddar cheese (optional)

Guacamole (optional)

Sour cream (optional)

Sliced ripe olives (optional)

1. Heat the oven to 350°F. Spray **10** (3-inch) muffin-pan cups with the cooking spray.

2. Wrap the tortillas between damp paper towels. Microwave on HIGH for 30 seconds or until the tortillas are warm. Fold **1** tortilla into thirds to form a cone shape. Press the tortilla cone, wide end down, into a muffin-pan cup. Repeat with the remaining tortillas, rewarming in the microwave as needed.

3. Bake for 5 minutes or until the tortilla cones are golden. Remove the tortillas from the pan and cool on wire racks.

4. Heat the pork, picante sauce and chipotle chile pepper in a 2-quart saucepan over medium heat until the mixture is hot and bubbling, stirring often.

5. Spoon **about ¼ cup** pork mixture into **each** tortilla cone. Top with the cheese, guacamole, sour cream or olives, if desired.

KITCHEN TIP: You can prepare the tortillas through the baking step up to 24 hours ahead of time and store them in an airtight container.

CIDER-BRAISED PORK

makes 8 servings

2 tablespoons olive oil, divided

1 boneless pork shoulder roast (4 to 5 pounds), trimmed

1 teaspoon salt, divided

1 teaspoon black pepper, divided

2 pounds yellow onions, cut in half and thinly sliced

2 tablespoons water

3 cups apple cider

1. Heat 1 tablespoon oil in Dutch oven over medium-high heat. Season pork with ½ teaspoon salt and ½ teaspoon pepper; add to Dutch oven. Cook about 6 minutes per side or until browned. Remove pork to large plate.

2. Preheat oven to 300°F. Add remaining 1 tablespoon oil, onions and ½ teaspoon salt to Dutch oven; cook 10 minutes, stirring frequently. Stir in water, scraping up any browned bits from bottom of pan. Reduce heat to medium. Cover and cook over medium heat 15 minutes or until onions are deep golden brown, stirring occasionally.

3. Stir in cider and remaining ½ teaspoon pepper. Return pork to Dutch oven with any juices accumulated on plate. Cover; bake 3 hours or until pork is fork-tender.

SIMPLE SHREDDED PORK TACOS

makes 6 servings

2 pounds boneless pork roast

1 cup salsa

1 can (4 ounces) diced mild green chiles, drained

½ teaspoon garlic salt

½ teaspoon black pepper

Corn or flour tortillas, warmed

Optional toppings: tomatillo salsa, sliced jalapeño peppers, sour cream, shredded cheese and/or shredded lettuce

SLOW COOKER DIRECTIONS

1. Place pork in bottom of slow cooker. Combine salsa, chiles, garlic salt and pepper in small bowl; stir to blend. Pour salsa mixture over pork.

2. Cover; cook on LOW 8 hours. Remove pork to large cutting board; shred with two forks. Stir shredded pork back into slow cooker to keep warm. Serve on warm tortillas with desired toppings.

CHORIZO HASH

makes 4 servings

2 unpeeled russet potatoes, cut into ½-inch pieces

3 teaspoons salt, divided

8 ounces uncooked Mexican chorizo sausage

1 yellow onion, chopped

½ red bell pepper, chopped (about ½ cup)

Fried, poached or scrambled eggs (optional)

Avocado slices (optional)

Fresh cilantro leaves (optional)

1. Fill medium saucepan half full with water. Add potatoes and 2 teaspoons salt; bring to a boil over high heat. Reduce heat to medium-low. Cook 8 minutes. (Potatoes will be firm.) Drain.

2. Meanwhile, remove and discard casing from chorizo. Crumble chorizo into large (12-inch) cast iron skillet; cook and stir over medium-high heat 5 minutes or until lightly browned. Add onion and bell pepper; cook and stir 4 minutes or until vegetables are softened.

3. Stir in potatoes and remaining 1 teaspoon salt; cook 10 to 15 minutes or until vegetables are tender and potatoes are lightly browned, stirring occasionally. Serve with eggs, if desired; garnish with avocado and cilantro.

SAUSAGE AND KALE DEEP-DISH MINI PIZZAS

makes 12 pizzas

1 tablespoon olive oil

4 ounces spicy pork Italian sausage

⅓ cup finely chopped red onion

2½ cups packed chopped stemmed kale

¼ teaspoon salt

1 loaf (16 ounces) frozen pizza dough or white bread dough, thawed according to package directions

¾ cup (3 ounces) shredded Italian blend cheese

¼ cup pizza sauce

1. Preheat oven to 400°F. Spray 12 standard (2½-inch) muffin pan cups with nonstick cooking spray.

2. Heat oil in large skillet over medium-high heat. (If using pork sausage, oil is not needed.) Remove sausage from casings; crumble into skillet. Cook and stir 5 minutes or until no longer pink. Remove to plate. Add onion to skillet; cook and stir 4 minutes or until softened. Add kale; cook 10 minutes or until tender, stirring occasionally. Return sausage to skillet with salt; stir until blended. Set aside to cool slightly.

3. Divide dough into 12 pieces. Stretch or roll each piece into 5-inch circle; press into prepared muffin cups. Sprinkle 1 teaspoon cheese into bottom of each cup; spread 1 teaspoon pizza sauce over cheese. Top evenly with kale mixture and remaining cheese.

4. Bake 16 minutes or until golden brown. Let stand in pan 1 minute; loosen sides with small spatula or knife. Remove to wire rack. Serve warm.

PORK AND SWEET POTATO SKILLET

makes 4 servings

1 tablespoon plus
 1 teaspoon butter,
 divided

¾ pound pork tenderloin,
 cut into 1-inch pieces

¼ teaspoon salt

⅛ teaspoon black pepper

2 medium sweet potatoes,
 peeled and cut into
 ½-inch pieces (about
 2 cups)

1 small onion, sliced

4 ounces smoked turkey
 sausage, halved
 lengthwise and cut
 into ½-inch pieces

1 small green or red apple,
 cut into ½-inch slices

½ cup sweet and sour
 sauce

2 tablespoons chopped
 fresh parsley
 (optional)

1. Heat 1 teaspoon butter in large nonstick skillet over medium-high heat. Add pork; cook and stir 2 to 3 minutes or until pork is no longer pink. Season with salt and pepper. Remove to plate.

2. Add remaining 1 tablespoon butter, sweet potatoes and onion to skillet; cover and cook over medium-low heat 8 to 10 minutes or until tender.

3. Add pork, sausage, apple and sweet and sour sauce to skillet; cook until heated through, stirring occasionally. Garnish with parsley.

GLAZED PORK CHOPS WITH CORN STUFFING

makes 6 servings

1¾ cups Swanson® Chicken Stock

⅛ teaspoon ground red pepper

1 cup frozen whole kernel corn

1 stalk celery, chopped (about ½ cup)

1 medium onion, chopped (about ½ cup)

4 cups Pepperidge Farm® Corn Bread Stuffing

Vegetable cooking spray

6 boneless pork chops, ¾-inch thick (about 1½ pounds)

2 tablespoons packed brown sugar

2 teaspoons spicy-brown mustard

1. Heat the stock, red pepper, corn, celery and onion in a 3-quart saucepan over medium heat to a boil. Remove the saucepan from the heat. Add the stuffing and mix lightly.

2. Spray a 3-quart shallow baking dish with the cooking spray. Spoon the stuffing into the baking dish. Top with the pork. Stir the brown sugar and mustard in a small bowl until the mixture is smooth. Spread the brown sugar mixture over the pork.

3. Bake at 400°F. for 30 minutes or until the pork is cooked through.

MU SHU PORK WRAPS

makes 4 servings

1 tablespoon dark sesame oil

1 red bell pepper, cut into short, thin strips

1 small pork tenderloin (¾ pound), cut into strips

1 medium zucchini or summer squash, or combination, cut into strips

3 cloves garlic, minced

2 cups prepared coleslaw mix or shredded cabbage

2 tablespoons hoisin sauce

4 (10-inch) wraps made with olive oil

¼ cup plum sauce

1. Heat oil in large deep nonstick skillet over medium-high heat. Add bell pepper; cook and stir 2 minutes. Add pork, zucchini and garlic; cook and stir 4 to 5 minutes or until pork is cooked through and vegetables are crisp-tender. Add coleslaw mix; cook and stir 2 minutes or until wilted. Add hoisin sauce; cook and stir 1 minute.

2. Heat wraps according to package directions. Spread plum sauce down centers of wraps; top with pork mixture. Roll up tightly; cut diagonally in half.

PORK CURRY OVER CAULIFLOWER COUSCOUS

makes 6 servings

3 tablespoons olive oil, divided

2 tablespoons mild curry powder

2 teaspoons minced garlic

1½ pounds boneless pork (shoulder, loin or chops), cubed

1 red or green bell pepper, diced

1 tablespoon cider vinegar

½ teaspoon salt

2 cups water

1 large head cauliflower

Fresh cilantro sprigs (optional)

1. Heat 2 tablespoons oil in large saucepan over medium heat. Add curry powder and garlic; cook and stir 1 to 2 minutes or until garlic is golden.

2. Add pork; cook and stir 5 to 7 minutes or until pork cubes are barely pink in center. Add bell pepper and vinegar; cook and stir 3 minutes or until bell pepper is soft. Sprinkle with salt.

3. Add water; bring to a boil. Reduce heat to low. Simmer 30 to 45 minutes or until liquid is reduced and pork is tender, stirring occasionally and adding additional water as needed.

4. Meanwhile, trim and core cauliflower; cut into equal pieces. Place in food processor; pulse until cauliflower is in small uniform pieces about the size of cooked couscous. *Do not purée.*

5. Heat remaining 1 tablespoon oil in large skillet over medium heat. Add cauliflower; cook and stir 5 minutes or until crisp-tender. *Do not overcook.* Serve pork curry over cauliflower. Garnish with cilantro.

SPICY CHICKEN RIGATONI

makes 4 servings

2 tablespoons olive oil

2 cloves garlic, minced

½ teaspoon red pepper flakes

½ teaspoon black pepper

8 ounces boneless skinless chicken breasts, cut into thin strips

1 cup marinara sauce

¾ cup Alfredo sauce

1 package (16 ounces) mezzo rigatoni, rigatoni or penne pasta, cooked until al dente

¾ cup frozen peas, thawed

Grated Parmesan cheese (optional)

1. Heat oil in large saucepan over medium-high heat. Add garlic, red pepper flakes and black pepper; cook and stir 1 minute. Add chicken; cook and stir 4 minutes or until cooked through.

2. Stir in marinara sauce and Alfredo sauce until blended. Reduce heat to medium-low. Cook 10 minutes, stirring occasionally.

3. Stir in pasta and peas; cook 2 minutes or until heated through. Sprinkle with cheese, if desired.

PASTA E FAGIOLI

makes 8 servings

2 tablespoons olive oil

1 cup chopped onion

3 cloves garlic, minced

2 cans (about 14 ounces each) Italian-style stewed tomatoes, undrained

3 cups chicken broth

1 can (about 15 ounces) cannellini beans (white kidney beans),* undrained

¼ cup chopped fresh Italian parsley

1 teaspoon dried basil

¼ teaspoon black pepper

4 ounces uncooked small shell pasta

If cannellini beans are unavailable, substitute Great Northern beans.

1. Heat oil in 4-quart Dutch oven over medium heat. Add onion and garlic; cook and stir 5 minutes or until onion is tender.

2. Add tomatoes, broth, beans with liquid, parsley, basil and pepper to Dutch oven; bring to a boil over high heat, stirring occasionally. Reduce heat to low. Cover; simmer 10 minutes.

3. Add pasta to Dutch oven. Cover; simmer 10 minutes or just until pasta is tender. Serve immediately.

ITALIAN CHEESEBURGER PASTA

makes 4 servings

1 pound ground beef

1 jar (1 pound 10 ounces) Prego® Traditional Italian Sauce

2 cups water

2 cups uncooked corkscrew-shaped pasta (rotini)

½ cup shredded mozzarella cheese

1. Cook the beef in a 10-inch skillet over medium-high heat until it's well browned, stirring frequently to separate the meat. Pour off any fat.

2. Stir the Italian sauce, water and pasta into the skillet. Heat to a boil. Reduce the heat to medium. Cook and stir for 25 minutes or until the pasta is tender but still firm. Sprinkle with the cheese.

SPAGHETTI & MEATBALLS

makes 4 servings

6 ounces uncooked multigrain or whole wheat spaghetti

¾ pound ground beef

¼ pound hot turkey Italian sausage, casing removed

1 egg white

2 tablespoons plain dry bread crumbs

1 teaspoon dried oregano

2 cups tomato-basil pasta sauce

3 tablespoons chopped fresh basil

2 tablespoons grated Parmesan cheese

1. Preheat oven to 450°F. Spray baking sheet with nonstick cooking spray. Cook spaghetti according to package directions, omitting salt and fat. Drain and keep warm.

2. Combine beef, sausage, egg white, bread crumbs and oregano in medium bowl; mix well. Shape mixture into 16 (1½-inch) meatballs. Place on prepared baking sheet; coat with cooking spray. Bake 12 minutes, turning once.

3. Pour pasta sauce into large skillet. Add meatballs; cook over medium heat 9 minutes or until sauce is heated through and meatballs are cooked through (160°F), stirring occasionally. Divide spaghetti among four plates. Top with meatballs and sauce; sprinkle with basil and cheese.

CREAMY CHICKEN FLORENTINE

makes 4 servings

1 can (10¾ ounces) Campbell's® Condensed Cream of Chicken Soup (Regular **or** 98% Fat Free)

1½ cups water

½ of a 20-ounce bag frozen cut leaf spinach, thawed and well drained (about 3½ cups)

1 can (about 14.5 ounces) Italian-style diced tomatoes

4 skinless, boneless chicken breast halves (about 1 pound), cut into 1-inch cubes

2½ cups **uncooked** penne pasta

½ cup shredded mozzarella cheese (about 2 ounces)

1. Heat the oven to 375°F. Stir the soup, water, spinach, tomatoes and chicken in a 3-quart shallow baking dish. Cover the baking dish.

2. Bake for 20 minutes. Cook the pasta according to the package directions and drain well in a colander. Uncover the baking dish and stir in the pasta.

3. Bake for 20 minutes or until the pasta mixture is hot and bubbling. Sprinkle with the cheese. Let stand for 5 minutes or until the cheese is melted.

HEARTY BEEF LASAGNA

makes 8 to 10 servings

1 pound ground beef

1 jar (32 ounces) pasta sauce

2 cups (16 ounces) cottage cheese

1 container (8 ounces) sour cream

8 uncooked lasagna noodles

1½ cups (6 ounces) shredded mozzarella cheese

½ cup grated Parmesan cheese

1 cup water

Fresh basil or thyme (optional)

1. Preheat oven to 350°F.

2. Brown beef in large skillet over medium-high heat 6 to 8 minutes, stirring to break up meat. Drain fat. Reduce heat to low. Add pasta sauce; cook and stir occasionally until heated through. Combine cottage cheese and sour cream in medium bowl; blend well.

3. Spread 1½ cups meat sauce in bottom of 13×9-inch baking pan. Place 4 uncooked noodles over sauce. Top with half of cottage cheese mixture, ¾ cup mozzarella cheese, half of remaining meat sauce and ¼ cup Parmesan cheese. Repeat layers starting with uncooked noodles and topping with remaining ¾ cup mozzarella cheese. Pour water around sides of pan. Cover tightly with foil.

4. Bake 1 hour. Remove foil. Bake, uncovered, 20 minutes or until hot and bubbly. Let stand 15 to 20 minutes before cutting into squares. Garnish with basil.

ZESTY CHICKEN & RED PEPPER PASTA

makes 4 servings

½ cup roasted red peppers, drained

1 can (4 ounces) mild green chilies, drained

3 cloves garlic, minced

2 boneless, skinless chicken breast halves, cut into 1-inch cubes

8 ounces fettuccine noodles, cooked and drained

½ cup sun-dried tomatoes, rehydrated and chopped

½ cup sliced green onions

2 cups (8 ounces) SARGENTO® Shredded Reduced Fat 4 Cheese Italian, divided

1. Combine red peppers and chilies in blender or food processor; process until smooth (add up to ¼ cup water or chicken broth while processing if mixture is too thick); set aside.

2. Coat large nonstick skillet with cooking spray. Add garlic; cook 30 seconds over medium-high heat, stirring constantly. Add chicken; cook 5 minutes, or until browned on all sides, stirring frequently.

3. Stir fettuccine, sauce, tomatoes and onions into chicken. Cook 5 minutes, or until heated through, stirring frequently. Remove from heat. Stir in 1½ cups cheese. Top individual servings evenly with remaining cheese.

POTATO GNOCCHI WITH TOMATO SAUCE

makes 4 servings

2 pounds baking potatoes (3 or 4 large)

Tomato Sauce (recipe follows)

⅔ to 1 cup all-purpose flour, divided

1 egg yolk

½ teaspoon salt

⅛ teaspoon ground nutmeg (optional)

Grated Parmesan cheese

Slivered fresh basil

1. Preheat oven to 425°F. Pierce potatoes several times with fork. Bake 1 hour or until soft. Meanwhile, prepare Tomato Sauce.

2. Cut potatoes in half lengthwise; cool slightly. Scoop out potatoes from skins into medium bowl; discard skins. Mash potatoes until smooth. Add ⅓ cup flour, egg yolk, salt and nutmeg, if desired; mix well to form dough.

3. Turn out dough onto well-floured surface. Knead in enough remaining flour to form smooth dough. Divide dough into four pieces; roll each piece with hands on lightly floured surface into ¾- to 1-inch-wide rope. Cut each rope into 1-inch pieces; gently press thumb into center of each piece to make indentation. Transfer gnocchi to lightly floured kitchen towel in single layer to prevent sticking.

4. Bring 4 quarts salted water to a gentle boil in large saucepan over high heat. To test cooking time, drop several into water; cook 1 minute or until they float to surface. Remove from water with slotted spoon and taste for doneness. (If gnocchi start to dissolve, reduce cooking time by several seconds.) Cook remaining gnocchi in batches, removing with slotted spoon to warm serving dish.

5. Serve gnocchi with Tomato Sauce; sprinkle with cheese and basil.

TOMATO SAUCE

makes about 2 cups

- 2 tablespoons olive oil or butter
- 1 clove garlic, minced
- 2 pounds ripe plum tomatoes, peeled, seeded and chopped
- 1 teaspoon sugar
- ¼ cup finely chopped prosciutto or cooked ham (optional)
- 1 tablespoon finely chopped fresh basil
- Salt and black pepper

Heat oil in medium saucepan over medium heat. Add garlic; cook 30 seconds or until fragrant. Stir in tomatoes and sugar; cook 10 minutes or until most liquid has evaporated. Stir in prosciutto, if desired, and basil; cook 2 minutes. Season to taste with salt and pepper.

BEEFY TORTELLINI

makes 6 servings

½ pound ground beef

1 jar (24 to 26 ounces) roasted tomato and garlic pasta sauce

1 package (12 ounces) uncooked three-cheese tortellini

8 ounces sliced button or exotic mushrooms, such as oyster, shiitake and cremini

½ cup water

½ teaspoon red pepper flakes (optional)

¾ cup grated Asiago or Romano cheese

Chopped fresh Italian parsley (optional)

SLOW COOKER DIRECTIONS

1. Coat inside of slow cooker with nonstick cooking spray. Brown beef in large skillet over medium-high heat 6 to 8 minutes, stirring to break up meat. Remove to slow cooker using slotted spoon.

2. Stir pasta sauce, tortellini, mushrooms, water and red pepper flakes, if desired, into slow cooker. Cover; cook on LOW 2 hours or on HIGH 1 hour. Stir.

3. Cover; cook on LOW 2 to 2½ hours or on HIGH ½ to 1 hour. Serve in shallow bowls topped with cheese and parsley, if desired.

CLASSIC ITALIAN PASTA SALAD

makes 8 side-dish servings

8 ounces rotelle or spiral pasta, cooked and drained

2½ cups assorted cut-up fresh vegetables (broccoli, carrots, tomatoes, bell peppers and onions)

½ cup cubed Cheddar or mozzarella cheese

⅓ cup sliced pitted ripe olives (optional)

1 cup WISH-BONE® Italian Dressing

Combine all ingredients except WISH-BONE® Italian Dressing in large bowl. Add Dressing; toss well. Serve chilled or at room temperature.

TIP: If preparing a day ahead, refrigerate, then stir in ¼ cup additional WISH-BONE® Dressing before serving.

VARIATION: For a Creamy Italian Pasta Salad, substitute ½ cup HELLMANN'S® or BEST FOODS® Real Mayonnaise for ½ cup WISH-BONE® Italian Dressing.

SUBSTITUTION: Also terrific with WISH-BONE® Robusto Italian, Fat Free! Italian, House Italian, Ranch, Light Ranch, Fat-Free! Ranch, Creamy Caesar, Red Wine Vinaigrette or Fat Free! Red Wine Vinaigrette Dressings.

6-CHEESE ITALIAN SAUSAGE & PASTA

makes 6 servings

1 pound mild or hot Italian sausage

1 large onion, coarsely chopped

2 cloves garlic, minced

1 each: large red and green bell peppers, cut into 1-inch squares

1 can (14½ ounces) diced tomatoes or Italian-style tomatoes, undrained

1 can (6 ounces) tomato paste

8 ounces ziti or mostaccioli pasta, cooked and drained

¼ cup chopped fresh basil or 2 teaspoons dried basil

2 cups (8 ounces) SARGENTO® Chef Blends™ Shredded 6 Cheese Italian, divided

1. Cut sausage into ½-inch pieces; discard casings. Cook sausage in large skillet over medium heat 5 minutes or until browned on all sides. Pour off drippings. Add onion, garlic and bell peppers; cook 5 minutes or until sausage is cooked through and vegetables are crisp-tender.

2. Add tomatoes and tomato paste; mix well. Stir in pasta, basil and 1 cup cheese. Transfer to 13×9-inch baking dish. Cover and bake in preheated 375°F oven 20 minutes. Uncover; sprinkle remaining cheese evenly over casserole. Continue to bake 5 minutes or until cheese is melted.

CILANTRO PEANUT PESTO ON SOBA

makes 1 cup pesto (4 to 6 servings)

1 cup packed fresh basil leaves

½ cup packed fresh cilantro leaves

¾ cup dry roasted peanuts, divided

1 jalapeño pepper, seeded

3 cloves garlic

2 teaspoons liquid aminos

1 tablespoon plus ¾ teaspoon salt, divided

½ cup peanut oil

1 package (about 12 ounces) uncooked soba noodles

Chopped fresh cilantro

1. Combine basil, ½ cup cilantro, ½ cup peanuts, jalapeño, garlic, liquid aminos and ¾ teaspoon salt in food processor; pulse until coarsely chopped. With motor running, drizzle in oil in thin, steady stream; process until well blended.

2. Bring large saucepan of water to a boil. Add remaining 1 tablespoon salt; stir until dissolved. Add noodles; return to a boil. Reduce heat to low. Cook 3 minutes or until tender. Drain and rinse under cold water to cool.

3. Place noodles in medium bowl; stir in pesto. Chop remaining ¼ cup peanuts; sprinkle over noodles. Garnish with chopped cilantro.

TOMATO, SPINACH AND FETA PASTA

makes 4 servings

6 ounces uncooked penne pasta (about 2 cups)

1 tablespoon extra virgin olive oil

1 teaspoon salt

8 ounces (about 1½ cups) cherry or grape tomatoes, halved

¾ cup cubed feta cheese

¼ cup fresh spinach leaves

1. Cook pasta according to package directions. Rinse under cold water. Drain. Toss with oil and salt.

2. Add tomatoes and cheese; toss to blend. Top with spinach.

CHICKEN BOWTIE PARTY

makes 4 servings

1 package (10 to 12 ounces) uncooked bowtie pasta

6 slices bacon, chopped

12 ounces boneless skinless chicken breasts, cut into 2×½-inch strips*

⅓ cup chopped red onion

1 teaspoon minced garlic

2 plum tomatoes, diced (about ½ cup)

1 cup whipping cream

¼ cup shredded Asiago cheese, plus additional for garnish

1 jar (15 ounces) Alfredo sauce

Finely chopped fresh parsley (optional)

Or substitute 12 ounces grilled chicken breast strips; add to skillet with tomatoes in step 3.

1. Cook pasta in large saucepan of salted boiling water until al dente. Drain and return to saucepan; keep warm.

2. Meanwhile, cook bacon in large skillet over medium-high heat until cooked through. (Bacon should still be chewy, not quite crisp.) Remove to paper towel-lined plate. Drain all but 1 tablespoon drippings from skillet.

3. Add chicken to skillet; cook 4 minutes or until chicken begins to brown, turning occasionally. Add onion and garlic; cook and stir 2 minutes. Add tomatoes and bacon; cook and stir 1 minute. Stir in cream and ¼ cup cheese; cook 4 minutes or until liquid is slightly reduced.

4. Add chicken mixture and Alfredo sauce to pasta in saucepan; stir gently to coat. Cook over medium heat until heated through, stirring occasionally. Garnish with parsley and additional cheese.

THREE-PEPPER FETTUCCINE

makes 4 servings

1 *each* grilled red bell pepper, yellow bell pepper and jalapeño pepper (see TIP)

1 tablespoon olive oil

½ teaspoon chopped fresh thyme *or* ¼ teaspoon dried thyme

⅛ teaspoon salt plus additional for cooking pasta

⅛ teaspoon black pepper

1 package (9 ounces) refrigerated fresh fettuccine

3 ounces mild goat cheese, crumbled

2 tablespoons minced fresh chives or green onions

1. Core and seed bell peppers; cut into thin strips. Place in large bowl. Core, seed and mince jalapeño. Add to bell peppers. Stir in oil, thyme, ⅛ teaspoon salt and black pepper.

2. Cook fettuccine according to package directions; drain well. Add fettuccine to peppers. Toss well. Add cheese. Toss again. Sprinkle with chives.

TIP: To grill peppers, broil on foil-lined baking sheet or broiler pan, turning occasionally, until peppers are charred all over. Place peppers in a bowl; cover with plastic wrap. Let steam at least 10 minutes. Remove charred skin. Proceed with recipe. Or, place peppers in a brown paper bag and close top. Let steam at least 10 minutes. Remove charred skin. Proceed with recipe. If desired, peppers can be grilled in advance and refrigerated.

STROGANOFF CASSEROLE

makes 8 servings

1 package (16 ounces) uncooked egg noodles

2 cans (10¾ ounces each) condensed cream of mushroom soup, undiluted

1 container (8 ounces) sour cream

½ cup milk

1 pound ground beef

2 cans (6 ounces each) sliced mushrooms, undrained

1 package (8 ounces) cream cheese

1 package (about 1 ounce) gravy mix

1. Preheat oven to 350°F. Cook noodles according to package directions in Dutch oven. Drain well; return to Dutch oven.

2. Add soups, sour cream and milk; mix well. Cover and keep warm.

3. Brown beef in large skillet over medium-high heat 6 to 8 minutes, stirring to break up meat. Drain fat. Add mushrooms, cream cheese and gravy mix to skillet; cook and stir until well blended. Add beef mixture to noodles in Dutch oven; stir gently to coat.

4. Bake 30 minutes or until heated through.

BOWTIE PASTA BOWL

makes 4 servings

3 cups chicken broth

6 ounces uncooked bowtie pasta

⅛ teaspoon red pepper flakes

1½ cups diced cooked chicken

1 medium tomato, seeded and diced

1 cup packed spring greens or spinach, coarsely chopped

3 tablespoons chopped fresh basil

⅛ teaspoon salt

1 cup (4 ounces) shredded mozzarella cheese

4 teaspoons grated Parmesan cheese

1. Bring broth to boil in large saucepan over high heat. Add pasta and red pepper flakes; return to a boil. Reduce heat to low. Cover and simmer 10 minutes or until pasta is al dente.

2. Add chicken; cook 1 minute. Remove from heat; stir in tomato, greens, basil and salt.

3. Spoon evenly into four shallow soup bowls; top evenly with mozzarella and Parmesan cheeses.

SERVING SUGGESTION: Serve with fresh slices of melon and iced tea with lemon and fresh mint.

SANTA FE ROTINI

makes 2 servings

- 3 ounces uncooked whole grain rotini pasta
- ½ of 15-ounce can black beans, rinsed and drained
- ⅓ cup finely chopped red onion
- 1 medium jalapeño pepper, seeded and chopped
- ¾ cup quartered grape tomatoes
- 1 tablespoon extra virgin olive oil
- ½ lime, cut into 4 wedges
- 1 clove garlic, minced
- ⅛ teaspoon salt
- 1 to 2 tablespoons chopped fresh cilantro

1. Cook pasta according to package directions omitting any salt or fat. Add beans during last minute of cooking. Drain.

2. Meanwhile, coat small skillet with nonstick cooking spray; heat over medium-high heat. Add onion and jalapeño; cook 2 minutes, stirring frequently. Add tomatoes; cook 2 minutes or until just tender, stirring frequently. Remove from heat. Cover; set aside.

3. In small bowl, combine oil, juice of 2 lime wedges, garlic and salt.

4. Place pasta mixture on two dinner plates. Stir oil mixture into tomato mixture until just coated; spoon evenly over pasta. Sprinkle evenly with cilantro. Serve with remaining lime wedges.

TIP: Freeze remaining beans in an airtight container for later use for up to 1 month.

Vegetables

COLORFUL COLESLAW

makes 4 to 6 servings

¼ head green cabbage, shredded or thinly sliced

¼ head red cabbage, shredded or thinly sliced

1 small yellow or orange bell pepper, thinly sliced

1 small jicama, peeled and julienned

¼ cup thinly sliced green onions

2 tablespoons chopped fresh cilantro

¼ cup vegetable oil

¼ cup fresh lime juice

1 teaspoon salt

⅛ teaspoon black pepper

1. Combine cabbage, bell pepper, jicama, green onions and cilantro in large bowl.

2. Whisk oil, lime juice, salt and black pepper in small bowl until well blended. Pour over vegetables; toss to coat. Cover; refrigerate 2 to 6 hours for flavors to blend.

NOTE: This coleslaw makes a great topping for tacos and sandwiches.

Vegetables

ITALIAN PRIMAVERA LUNCH-BOX EXPRESS >>

makes 1 serving

1 cup frozen vegetable
   blend (broccoli, carrots
   and cauliflower),
   thawed
¾ cup chunky garden-
   style pasta sauce
¼ teaspoon Italian
   seasoning
1 cup cooked brown rice
   Grated Parmesan
   cheese (optional)

MICROWAVE DIRECTIONS

1. Combine vegetables, pasta sauce and Italian seasoning in 1-quart microwavable bowl. Cover with vented plastic wrap. Microwave on HIGH 1 to 1½ minutes or until heated through; stir.

2. Microwave rice on HIGH 1 to 1½ minutes or until heated through. Top with vegetable mixture and cheese, if desired.

BACON-ROASTED BRUSSELS SPROUTS

makes 4 servings

1 pound Brussels sprouts
3 slices bacon, cut into
   ½-inch pieces
2 teaspoons packed
   brown sugar
   Salt and black pepper

1. Preheat oven to 400°F. Trim ends from Brussels sprouts; cut in half lengthwise.

2. Combine Brussels sprouts, bacon and brown sugar in glass baking dish.

3. Roast 25 to 30 minutes or until golden brown, stirring once. Season with salt and pepper.

CIDER VINAIGRETTE-GLAZED BEETS

makes 8 servings

6 medium beets

1 tablespoon olive oil

1 tablespoon cider vinegar

½ teaspoon prepared horseradish

½ teaspoon Dijon mustard

¼ teaspoon packed brown sugar

⅓ cup crumbled blue cheese (optional)

1. Cut tops off beets, leaving at least 1 inch of stems. Scrub beets under running water with soft vegetable brush, being careful not to break skins. Place beets in large saucepan; add water to cover. Bring to a boil over high heat. Reduce heat to low. Simmer 30 minutes or just until beets are barely firm when pierced with fork. Remove to plate to cool slightly.

2. Meanwhile, whisk oil, vinegar, horseradish, mustard and brown sugar in medium bowl until well blended.

3. When beets are cool enough to handle, peel off skins and trim off root end. Cut beets into halves, then into wedges. Add warm beets to vinaigrette; gently toss to coat. Sprinkle with cheese, if desired. Serve warm or at room temperature.

KALE WITH LEMON AND GARLIC

makes 8 servings

2 bunches kale or Swiss chard (1 to 1¼ pounds)

1 tablespoon olive or vegetable oil

3 cloves garlic, minced

½ cup chicken or vegetable broth

½ teaspoon salt

¼ teaspoon black pepper

1 lemon, cut into 8 wedges

1. Trim any tough stems from kale. Stack and thinly slice leaves. Heat oil in large saucepan over medium heat. Add garlic; cook 3 minutes, stirring occasionally. Add chopped kale and broth; cover and simmer 7 minutes. Stir kale; cover and simmer over medium-low heat 8 to 10 minutes or until kale is tender.

2. Season with salt and pepper. Squeeze wedge of lemon over each serving.

TWO-TONED STUFFED POTATOES

makes 6 servings

3 large baking potatoes (12 ounces each)

2 large sweet potatoes (12 ounces each), dark flesh preferred

3 slices thick-cut bacon, cut in half crosswise diagonally

2 cups chopped onions

⅔ cup buttermilk

¼ cup (½ stick) butter, cut into small pieces

¾ teaspoon salt, divided

1. Preheat oven to 450°F. Pierce potatoes with fork in several places. Bake directly on rack 45 minutes or until fork-tender. Let potatoes stand until cool enough to handle. *Reduce oven temperature to 350°F.*

2. Meanwhile, cook bacon in medium skillet over medium-high heat 6 to 8 minutes or until crisp. Remove bacon to paper towels using slotted spoon.

3. Add onions to drippings in skillet; cook 12 minutes over medium-high heat or until golden brown. Remove onions from skillet; set aside. Stir buttermilk into skillet, scraping up any browned bits from bottom of skillet. Add butter; stir until melted.

4. Cut baking potatoes in half lengthwise with serrated knife; scoop out flesh into large bowl. Reserve skins. Add three fourths buttermilk mixture, ½ teaspoon salt and three fourths onions to bowl. Mash with potato masher until smooth.

5. Cut sweet potatoes in half lengthwise with serrated knife; scoop out flesh into medium bowl. Discard skins. Add remaining one fourth buttermilk mixture, ¼ teaspoon salt and one fourth onions to sweet potatoes. Mash with potato masher until smooth.

6. Fill half of each reserved potato skin horizontally, vertically or diagonally with baked potato mixture; fill other half with sweet potato mixture. Top each stuffed potato half with bacon slice. Transfer stuffed potatoes to baking sheet; bake 15 minutes or until heated through.

CAULIFLOWER WITH ONION BUTTER

makes 8 to 10 servings

½ cup (1 stick) butter, divided

1 cup diced onion

1 large head cauliflower, broken into florets

½ cup water

1. Melt ¼ cup butter in medium skillet over medium heat. Add onion; cook 20 minutes or until onion is deep golden brown, stirring occasionally.

2. Meanwhile, place cauliflower and water in microwavable bowl. Microwave on HIGH 8 minutes or until crisp-tender; drain, if necessary.

3. Add remaining ¼ cup butter to skillet with onion; cook and stir until butter is melted. Pour over cooked cauliflower; serve immediately.

GRILLED POTATO SALAD

makes 4 servings

¼ cup country-style Dijon mustard

2 tablespoons chopped fresh dill

1 tablespoon white wine vinegar or cider vinegar

1½ teaspoons salt, divided

¼ teaspoon black pepper

5 tablespoons olive oil, divided

8 cups water

2 pounds small red potatoes

1 green onion, thinly sliced

1. Prepare grill for direct cooking.

2. Whisk mustard, dill, vinegar, ½ teaspoon salt and pepper in measuring cup. Gradually whisk in 3 tablespoons oil. Set aside.

3. Bring water and remaining 1 teaspoon salt to a boil in large saucepan over medium-high heat. Cut potatoes into ½-inch slices. Add potatoes to saucepan; boil 5 minutes. Drain; return potatoes to saucepan. Drizzle with remaining 2 tablespoons oil; toss lightly.

4. Spray one side of large foil sheet with nonstick cooking spray. Transfer potatoes to foil; fold into packet. Place potato packet on grid. Grill 10 minutes or until potatoes are tender. Transfer potatoes to serving bowl. Sprinkle with green onion. Add dressing and toss gently to coat. Serve warm.

COLA CHUTNEY CARROTS >>

makes 4 servings

2 cups baby carrots

1 can (12 ounces) cola beverage

1 cup water plus additional, as needed

3 tablespoons cranberry chutney

1 tablespoon Dijon mustard

2 teaspoons butter

2 tablespoons chopped pecans, toasted

1. Place carrots in medium saucepan over medium-high heat; cover with cola and 1 cup water. Bring to a boil, reduce heat and simmer until carrots are tender, about 8 minutes.

2. Drain carrots and return to saucepan. Add chutney, mustard and butter; cook and stir 4 to 6 minutes over medium-low heat until carrots are glazed.

3. Place carrots in serving bowl. Top with pecans.

NOTE: Mango chutney can be used in place of cranberry chutney.

COUNTRY-STYLE CORN

makes 6 to 8 servings

4 slices bacon

1 tablespoon all-purpose flour

1 can (about 15 ounces) corn, drained

1 can (about 15 ounces) cream-style corn

1 red bell pepper, diced

½ cup sliced green onions

Salt and black pepper

1. Cook bacon in large skillet over medium heat until crisp; drain on paper towels. Crumble bacon; set aside.

2. Whisk flour into drippings in skillet. Add corn, cream-style corn and bell pepper; bring to a boil. Reduce heat to low. Cook 10 minutes or until thickened.

3. Stir green onions and bacon into corn mixture. Season with salt and black pepper.

STEAKHOUSE CREAMED SPINACH

makes 4 servings

1 pound baby spinach

½ cup (1 stick) butter

2 tablespoons finely chopped onion

¼ cup all-purpose flour

2 cups whole milk

1 bay leaf

½ teaspoon salt

Pinch ground nutmeg

Pinch ground red pepper

Black pepper

1. Heat medium saucepan of water to a boil over high heat. Add spinach; cook 1 minute. Drain and transfer to bowl of ice water to stop cooking. Squeeze spinach dry; coarsely chop. Wipe out saucepan with paper towel.

2. Melt butter in same saucepan over medium heat. Add onion; cook and stir 2 minutes or until softened. Add flour; cook and stir 2 to 3 minutes or until slightly golden. Slowly add milk in thin, steady stream, whisking constantly until mixture boils and begins to thicken. Stir in bay leaf, ½ teaspoon salt, nutmeg and red pepper. Reduce heat to low. Cook and stir 5 minutes. Remove and discard bay leaf.

3. Stir in spinach; cook 5 minutes, stirring frequently. Season with additional salt and black pepper.

BRAISED BRUSSELS SPROUTS WITH CARAMELIZED ONIONS

makes 4 servings

1½ teaspoons butter

1 cup diced onion

5 tablespoons cola beverage, divided

1 teaspoon balsamic vinegar

1 pound Brussels sprouts, trimmed and halved lengthwise

3 tablespoons dry white wine, divided

Salt and black pepper

1. Heat butter in large skillet over medium heat. Reduce heat to medium-low. Add onion; cook 10 minutes. Add 1 tablespoon cola and vinegar; cook 5 minutes.

2. Cook Brussels sprouts in boiling water, in medium saucepan 5 minutes; drain. Add Brussels sprouts to skillet with onion. Increase heat to medium. Add 2 tablespoons wine and 2 tablespoons cola; cook 3 minutes or until most liquid has evaporated from skillet.

3. Add remaining 1 tablespoon wine and 2 tablespoons cola to skillet; stir and cook 2 minutes or until most liquid has evaporated from skillet and Brussels sprouts are tender. Season with salt and pepper.

NOTE: The caramelized onions add a tasty touch to these bright green vegetables.

DELICIOUS CORN SOUFFLÉ

makes 6 servings

3 tablespoons all-purpose flour

1 tablespoon sugar

½ teaspoon black pepper

3 eggs

2 cups frozen whole kernel corn, thawed and drained

1 can (about 15 ounces) cream-style corn

1 cup (4 ounces) shredded Mexican cheese blend or Monterey Jack cheese

1 jar (2 ounces) chopped pimientos, drained

⅓ cup milk

1. Preheat oven to 350°F. Spray 8-inch round baking dish with nonstick cooking spray.

2. Combine flour, sugar and pepper in large bowl. Add eggs; beat with electric mixer at high speed until smooth. Stir in corn kernels, cream-style corn, cheese, pimientos and milk. Pour into prepared baking dish.

3. Bake, uncovered, 55 minutes or until set. Let stand 15 minutes before serving.

ASIAN-GLAZED ROASTED ASPARAGUS

makes 4 servings

3 tablespoons cola beverage, divided

1 tablespoon plus 1 teaspoon soy sauce, divided

1 tablespoon dry white wine

1 teaspoon packed brown sugar

1 clove garlic, minced

1 teaspoon cornstarch

1 pound asparagus, ends trimmed

1 tablespoon olive oil

Salt and black pepper

Toasted sesame seeds

Shredded Cheddar cheese (optional)

1. Preheat oven to 375°F. Combine 2 tablespoons cola, 1 tablespoon soy sauce, wine, brown sugar, garlic and cornstarch in small bowl. Set aside.

2. Toss asparagus with oil, remaining 1 tablespoon cola and 1 teaspoon soy sauce on rimmed baking sheet, then season with salt and pepper. Bake 10 to 12 minutes or until asparagus is crisp-tender.

3. Heat large skillet over medium-high heat. Add asparagus and sauce to skillet; stir to coat. When sauce has thickened, remove from heat and serve. Sprinkle with toasted sesame seeds and cheese, if desired.

TIP: When selecting asparagus, look for firm, smooth green stems with tightly closed tips; tips that are open are a sign of age. Look for even green shading along the whole length; ends that become lighter in color may be a sign of toughness. Avoid wilted spears and asparagus that has a strong odor.

STIR-FRY VEGETABLE PIZZA

makes 4 servings

1 pound (about 5 cups) fresh cut stir-fry vegetables (packaged or from the salad bar) such as broccoli, zucchini, bell peppers and red onions

1 (12-inch) prepared pizza crust

⅓ cup pizza sauce

¼ teaspoon red pepper flakes (optional)

1½ cups (6 ounces) shredded part-skim mozzarella cheese

1. Heat oven to 425°F.

2. Heat large nonstick skillet over medium-high heat 1 minute; coat with nonstick cooking spray. Add vegetables; stir-fry 4 to 5 minutes or until crisp-tender.

3. Place pizza crust on large baking sheet; top with pizza sauce. Sprinkle red pepper flakes over sauce, if desired. Arrange vegetables over sauce; top with cheese.

4. Bake 12 to 14 minutes or until crust is golden brown and cheese is melted. Cut into wedges.

TABBOULEH IN TOMATO CUPS

makes 4 main-dish or 8 side-dish servings

4 large firm ripe tomatoes (about 8 ounces each)

2 tablespoons olive oil

4 green onions with tops, thinly sliced diagonally

1 cup uncooked bulgur wheat

1 cup water

2 tablespoons lemon juice

1 tablespoon chopped fresh mint leaves *or* ½ teaspoon dried mint

Salt and black pepper

Lemon peel and fresh mint leaves (optional)

1. Cut tomatoes in half crosswise. Scoop pulp and seeds out of tomatoes into medium bowl, leaving ¼-inch-thick shells.

2. Invert tomatoes on paper towel-lined plate; drain 20 minutes. Chop tomato pulp; set aside.

3. Heat oil in medium saucepan over medium-high heat. Cook and stir white parts of green onions 1 to 2 minutes or until wilted. Add bulgur; cook 3 to 5 minutes or until browned.

4. Add reserved tomato pulp, water, lemon juice and 1 tablespoon chopped mint to bulgur mixture. Bring to a boil over high heat; reduce heat to medium-low. Cover; simmer gently 15 to 20 minutes until liquid is absorbed.

5. Set aside a few sliced green onion tops for garnish; stir remaining green onions into bulgur mixture. Season with salt and pepper. Spoon mixture into tomato cups.

6. Preheat oven to 400°F. Place filled cups in 13×9-inch baking dish; bake 15 minutes or until heated through. Top with reserved green onion tops. Garnish with lemon peel and mint leaves. Serve immediately.

CREAMY SLAB POTATOES

makes 4 servings

¼ cup (½ stick) butter, melted

1 teaspoon salt

½ teaspoon dried rosemary

½ teaspoon dried thyme

¼ teaspoon black pepper

2½ pounds Yukon Gold potatoes, peeled and cut crosswise into 1-inch slices (6 to 8 potatoes)

1 cup water

3 cloves garlic, smashed

1. Preheat oven to 500°F.

2. Combine butter, salt, rosemary, thyme and pepper in 13×9-inch baking pan (do not use glass); mix well. Add potatoes; toss to coat. Spread in single layer.

3. Bake 15 minutes. Turn potatoes; bake 15 minutes. Add water and garlic to pan; bake 15 minutes. Remove to serving plate; pour any remaining liquid in pan over potatoes.

BLACK BEAN & CORN RANCH SALAD

makes 5 servings

- ½ cup WISH-BONE® Light Ranch Dressing
- 1 can (about 15 ounces) reduced-sodium black beans, rinsed and drained
- 1 can (11 ounces) whole kernel corn or mexi-corn, drained
- 1 cup quartered grape or cherry tomatoes
- ½ cup chopped red onion
- 2 tablespoons chopped fresh cilantro
- Hot pepper sauce (optional)
- Lime wedges (optional)

Combine all ingredients in medium bowl. Serve chilled or at room temperature. Garnish with lime wedges.

CRISPY SMASHED POTATOES

makes about 6 servings

1 tablespoon plus ½ teaspoon salt, divided

3 pounds unpeeled small red potatoes (2 inches or smaller)

4 tablespoons (½ stick) butter, melted, divided

¼ teaspoon black pepper

½ cup grated Parmesan cheese (optional)

1. Fill large saucepan three-fourths full of water; add 1 tablespoon salt. Bring to a boil over high heat. Add potatoes; boil 20 minutes or until potatoes are tender when pierced with tip of sharp knife. Drain potatoes; set aside until cool enough to handle.

2. Preheat oven to 450°F. Brush baking sheet with 2 tablespoons butter. Working with one potato at a time, smash with hand or bottom of measuring cup to about ½-inch thickness. Arrange smashed potatoes in single layer on prepared baking sheet. Brush with remaining 2 tablespoons butter; sprinkle with remaining ½ teaspoon salt and pepper.

3. Bake 30 to 40 minutes or until bottoms of potatoes are golden brown. Turn potatoes; bake 10 minutes. Sprinkle with cheese, if desired; bake 5 minutes or until cheese is melted.

SCALLOPED TOMATOES & CORN

makes 4 to 6 servings

1 can (about 15 ounces) cream-style corn

1 can (about 14 ounces) diced tomatoes

¾ cup saltine cracker crumbs

1 egg, lightly beaten

2 teaspoons sugar

¾ teaspoon black pepper

Chopped fresh tomatoes (optional)

Chopped fresh Italian parsley (optional)

SLOW COOKER DIRECTIONS

1. Combine corn, diced tomatoes, cracker crumbs, egg, sugar and pepper in slow cooker; mix well.

2. Cover; cook on LOW 4 to 6 hours. Sprinkle with tomatoes and parsley before serving, if desired.

BROCCOLI-RICE CASSEROLE

makes 6 servings

½ cup chopped onion

½ cup chopped celery

⅓ cup chopped red bell pepper

1 can (10¾ ounces) condensed broccoli and cheese soup, undiluted

¼ cup sour cream

2 cups cooked rice

1 package (10 ounces) frozen chopped broccoli, thawed and drained

1 tomato, cut into ¼-inch-thick slices

1. Preheat oven to 350°F. Spray 1½-quart baking dish with nonstick cooking spray.

2. Coat large skillet with cooking spray; heat over medium heat. Add onion, celery and bell pepper; cook and stir 6 minutes or until crisp-tender. Stir in soup and sour cream. Layer rice and broccoli in prepared baking dish. Top evenly with soup mixture.

3. Bake, covered, 20 minutes. Top with tomato slices. Bake, uncovered, 10 minutes.

Index

Index

Acknowledgments

The publisher would like to thank the companies listed below for the use of their recipes and photographs in this publication.

Campbell Soup Company
McCormick® & Company, Inc.
Ortega®, A Division of B&G Foods North America, Inc.
Pinnacle Foods
Sargento® Foods Inc.

Metric Conversion Chart

VOLUME MEASUREMENTS (dry)

⅛ teaspoon = 0.5 mL
¼ teaspoon = 1 mL
½ teaspoon = 2 mL
¾ teaspoon = 4 mL
1 teaspoon = 5 mL
1 tablespoon = 15 mL
2 tablespoons = 30 mL
¼ cup = 60 mL
⅓ cup = 75 mL
½ cup = 125 mL
⅔ cup = 150 mL
¾ cup = 175 mL
1 cup = 250 mL
2 cups = 1 pint = 500 mL
3 cups = 750 mL
4 cups = 1 quart = 1 L

VOLUME MEASUREMENTS (fluid)

1 fluid ounce (2 tablespoons) = 30 mL
4 fluid ounces (½ cup) = 125 mL
8 fluid ounces (1 cup) = 250 mL
12 fluid ounces (1½ cups) = 375 mL
16 fluid ounces (2 cups) = 500 mL

WEIGHTS (mass)

½ ounce = 15 g
1 ounce = 30 g
3 ounces = 90 g
4 ounces = 120 g
8 ounces = 225 g
10 ounces = 285 g
12 ounces = 360 g
16 ounces = 1 pound = 450 g

DIMENSIONS

1/16 inch = 2 mm
⅛ inch = 3 mm
¼ inch = 6 mm
½ inch = 1.5 cm
¾ inch = 2 cm
1 inch = 2.5 cm

OVEN TEMPERATURES

250°F = 120°C
275°F = 140°C
300°F = 150°C
325°F = 160°C
350°F = 180°C
375°F = 190°C
400°F = 200°C
425°F = 220°C
450°F = 230°C

BAKING PAN SIZES

Utensil	Size in Inches/Quarts	Metric Volume	Size in Centimeters
Baking or Cake Pan (square or rectangular)	8×8×2	2 L	20×20×5
	9×9×2	2.5 L	23×23×5
	12×8×2	3 L	30×20×5
	13×9×2	3.5 L	33×23×5
Loaf Pan	8×4×3	1.5 L	20×10×7
	9×5×3	2 L	23×13×7
Round Layer Cake Pan	8×1½	1.2 L	20×4
	9×1½	1.5 L	23×4
Pie Plate	8×1¼	750 mL	20×3
	9×1¼	1 L	23×3
Baking Dish or Casserole	1 quart	1 L	—
	1½ quart	1.5 L	—
	2 quart	2 L	—